THE CROSS

a division of 10ofthose.com

The Cross
© Andrew Sach and Steve Jeffery, 2012

All rights reserved. Except as may be permitted by the Copyright Act, no part of this publication may be reproduced in any form or by any means without prior permission from the publisher.

Published by 10Publishing, a division of 10ofThose Limited

ISBN: 978-1-906173-59-3

All Scripture quotations are taken from THE HOLY BIBLE, NEW INTERNATIONAL VERSION®, NIV® Copyright © 1973, 1978, 1984 by Biblica, Inc.™ Used by permission. All rights reserved worldwide.

Cover Design by: Dan Collins
Typeset by: Diane Bainbridge

Printed in the UK.

10Publishing, a division of 10ofthose.com
Unit 19 Common Bank Industrial Estate, Ackhurst Road, Chorley, PR7 1NH, England.

Email: info@10ofthose.com
Website: www.10ofthose.com

Andrew Sach & Steve Jeffery

'WHEN THE TIME HAD FULLY COME'
THE CROSS AT THE CENTRE OF HISTORY

The cross of Christ stands at the centre of human history and at the heart of the gospel. 'When the time had fully come,' said the apostle Paul, 'God sent his Son' (Galatians 4:4). It is breathtaking to think that the eternal Son of God could become man, that the creator of heaven and earth could be formed as a tiny embryo in the womb of an unmarried mother. Yet the manger at Bethlehem was not the climax of his mission. It was not for another three decades, nailed to a Roman cross, that Christ could say, 'It is finished' (John 19:30).

Today the cross is one of the world's most recognizable symbols, the unmistakeable sign of the Christian faith. It is strange that the church should have chosen this as its emblem. Imagine how disgusted we would be to find in a jewellery shop an array of little gold electric chairs and silver hangman's nooses. Yet around our necks many of us wear an instrument of execution far more barbaric than either of these.

Crucifixion was one of the most brutal forms of torture ever devised, a shameful death reserved for the worst criminals. The condemned man was stripped of his clothing and forced to carry his cross through the streets, taunted by onlookers. No wonder the early Christians were ridiculed for their devotion to a Messiah who died in this way. A famous piece of graffiti dating from the third century depicts a man raising his hand to a crucified figure bearing the head of a donkey. 'Alexamenos worships his god,' mocks the inscription.

Yet the apostle Paul was not ashamed. Among the sophisticated intellectuals of first-century Corinth, he 'resolved to know nothing … except Jesus Christ and him crucified' (1 Corinthians 2:2). 'May I never boast', he told the Galatian churches, 'except in the cross of our Lord Jesus Christ' (Galatians 6:14). Neither has the Christian church through the ages been ashamed. Whenever we meet to celebrate the Lord's Supper, we 'proclaim the Lord's death until he comes' (1 Corinthians 11:26).

Christians do not love the cross because of a macabre fascination with death. We love it because it *means* something, because Christ *accomplished* something. Christ bore our punishment, securing our forgiveness. Christ defeated Satan, conquering our enemy. Christ set us an example, showing us both how to endure persecution and how to serve others. Through faith in him, we ourselves die and rise again, and so are liberated to live new lives. Like pieces of a jigsaw, these aspects of Christ's work fit together to form a single glorious picture. In this booklet we shall explore the different pieces in turn.

'PIERCED FOR OUR TRANSGRESSIONS' CHRIST PUNISHED IN OUR PLACE

The prophet Isaiah, writing centuries before Christ, spoke of one who would be 'pierced for our transgressions' (Isaiah 53:5). We will only understand his message if we first grasp the terrible predicament we find ourselves in.

Sin makes God angry. Some people have tried to deny this, insisting that there is no room for wrath in a God of love. But their view is possible only by taking a pair of scissors to the pages of

Scripture. The Bible affirms that 'God is love' (1 John 4:8,16), but it speaks no less clearly about of the terror of his judgment. Jesus spoke about hell more than anyone else in the Bible.

Now certainly God's anger is far removed from ours. He never loses his temper, nor is his anger ever malicious or spiteful. Rather, as John Stott notes, it is 'always predictable, because it is provoked by evil and by evil alone.'[1]

But that does not mean the wrath of God is reserved only for particularly bad people, such as Stalin or Mao. The Bible declares that all of us have rebelled against our Creator: 'There is no one righteous, not even one; there is no one who understands, no one who seeks God. All have turned away, they have together become worthless; there is no one who does good, not even one' (Romans 3:10–12). All of us are guilty. All of us stand under the wrath of God.[2]

If our predicament were merely ignorance, then enlightenment would be enough. If we lacked only motivation, an inspiring example might stir us. If we were simply enslaved by an external power, then a conquest would suffice. But we were 'God's enemies' and 'objects of wrath' (Romans 5:10; Ephesians 2:3). His holiness forbids unclean people like us from approaching Him. His justice demands our condemnation. We could not hope to rescue ourselves.

Wonderfully, God Himself has provided a solution. God became man in the LORD Jesus Christ, and suffered the punishment we deserved. This teaching is sometimes known as the doctrine of *penal substitution*. Jesus' death was 'penal' – He received God's punishment for sin. Jesus' death was a 'substitution' – He died in our place. Christ endured and exhausted God's wrath against His people on the cross of Calvary, so that we will not bear it ourselves.

This teaching has become unpopular in some circles, and is increasingly under attack. It is therefore essential that we be equipped to defend it. Let us look at three of the occasions where penal substitution is taught in Scripture.

Our first example takes us back to the sixth century BC. In 586–7 BC, Jerusalem fell to the Babylonians. King Zedekiah was blinded and deported, along with many of the leading citizens. Others, including the king's sons, were executed. This was a national catastrophe by any measure, but the Bible's explanation for what happened is even more terrifying: Israel's exile was God's punishment for their unrepentant sin.[3]

It was in the context of this impending exile that Isaiah prophesied about someone he called the 'Servant of the LORD'. In one of the most famous passages in the Old Testament, he explains that the Servant would offer himself as a penal substitutionary sacrifice, bearing the punishment due to God's people in their place.

Isaiah emphasizes throughout the appalling suffering the Servant endured: 'he was pierced … he was crushed … He was oppressed and afflicted … he was stricken … he poured out his life unto death' (Isaiah 53:5,7,8,12). But unlike the people of Israel, the Servant 'had done no violence, nor was any deceit in his mouth' (v. 9). His suffering therefore seems perplexing, particularly given Isaiah's insistence that 'it was the LORD's will to crush him and cause him to suffer' (v. 10). Israel deserved the punishment of exile, but why should the 'righteous Servant' (v. 11) suffer in this way?

Isaiah explains it like this:

> *He was pierced for our transgressions, he was*
> *crushed for our iniquities, the punishment*
> *that brought us peace was upon him, and by*
> *his wounds we are healed. We all, like sheep,*
> *have gone astray, each of us has turned to*
> *his own way, and the LORD has laid on him*
> *the iniquity of us all.* (Isaiah 53:5,6).

The Servant suffered not for his own sins, but for the sins of others. That is the point made repeatedly by the alternating pronouns ('he', 'our', 'him', 'us'). Isaiah twice uses the language of 'bearing' sin or iniquity (vv. 11,12), an expression which in the original Hebrew also carries connotations of receiving the punishment due to sin.[4]

In addition, the description of the Servant as a 'guilt offering' (v. 10) alludes to the atoning sacrifices of Leviticus 5 – 7, which God had prescribed to deal with sin. The writer to the Hebrews later explains that these sacrifices were not effective in themselves, for 'it is impossible for the blood of bulls and goats to take away sins' (Hebrews 10:4). Rather, they pointed ahead to the death of the LORD Jesus, who fulfilled them.

Ultimately only a human being could be a fit substitute for other human beings.

Thus the Servant's suffering was a source of hope for the exiled Israelites. Through his punishment and wounds, they received healing and peace. He did not merely join with them in their affliction. He bore the punishment they deserved in their place, in order that they might be spared.

The New Testament writers saw in Isaiah's Servant an explanation for Jesus' death.[5] 1 Peter 2:24,25 is particularly clear:

He himself bore our sins in his body on the tree, so that we might die to sins and live for righteousness; by his wounds you have been healed. For you were like sheep going astray, but now you have returned to the Shepherd and Overseer of your souls.

The language of straying sheep and wounds being healed is taken from Isaiah 53, and Peter affirms Isaiah's emphasis on sin-bearing ('He bore our sins') and substitution ('you' are healed by 'his' wounds). Peter does not explicitly quote Isaiah's statement about 'punishment', but relies on his readers' knowledge of Deuteronomy to make the same point. When he describes the cross as a 'tree', he echoes Deuteronomy 21:23: 'anyone who is hung on a tree is under God's curse'. Thus Peter teaches that Jesus suffered the curse due to God's people in their place.[6]

Our second example takes us to Mark's Gospel, and one of the most harrowing scenes in the Bible: the Garden of Gethsemane. Throughout Jesus' ministry we have seen Him calmly in control. He does not panic in a life-threatening storm, but stills it with a word. He is not worried by a food shortage, but multiplies bread to feed 5,000. And yet here, in Gethsemane, this same all-powerful Jesus is 'overwhelmed with sorrow to the point of death,' (Mark 14:34). Though He remained determinedly submitted to His Father's will, He nonetheless prayed, 'Take this cup from me' (Mark 14:36).

The reason for Jesus' anguish becomes clear when we understand what 'cup' He has in mind. Isaiah speaks of those who have 'drunk from the hand of the LORD the cup of his wrath … the goblet that makes men stagger' (Isaiah 51:17). Ezekiel describes it as a 'cup of ruin and desolation' (Ezekiel 23:33). Those who drink of it 'are filled with the wrath of the LORD and the rebuke of [their] God' (Isaiah 51:20). Jesus knew that He must soon face the wrath of His Father.

As Jesus cried out from the cross, 'My God, my God, why have you forsaken me?' (Mark 15:34), a terrible supernatural darkness covered the whole land. Darkness in the Old Testament symbolizes God's anger, for example in this passage which was in Jesus' mind the week before he died (he quotes from it in Mark 13:24):

> *See, the day of the LORD is coming – a cruel day, with wrath and fierce anger ... The stars of heaven and their constellations will not show their light. The rising sun will be darkened and the moon will not give its light. I will punish the world for its evil, the wicked for their sins.* (Isaiah 13:9–11)[7]

But why must Jesus, the innocent one, drink the cup reserved for 'the wicked of the earth' (Psalm 75:8)? Why is he God-forsaken, facing the darkness of God's judgment? He answered this question Himself earlier in Mark's Gospel, just after predicting His death for the third time: 'the Son of Man did not come to be served, but to serve, and to give His life as a ransom for many' (Mark 10:45). What extraordinary love our LORD has shown, that He should give His life in payment for ours, that He should willingly drink the cup of wrath reserved for us:

> *In Christ alone, who took on flesh,*
> *Fullness of God in helpless babe!*
> *This gift of love and righteousness,*
> *Scorned by the ones He came to save.*
> *Till on that cross as Jesus died,*
> *The wrath of God was satisfied;*
> *For every sin on Him was laid—*
> *Here in the death of Christ I live.*[8]

Keith Getty / Stuart Townend, © 2001 Thankyou Music

For our third and final example, we turn to the book of Numbers. When God rescued the Israelites from slavery in Egypt, He promised to lead them to a land flowing with milk and honey, but they complained that He had brought them up out of Egypt 'to die in the desert' (Numbers 21:5). He fed them with bread from heaven, but they grumbled about the 'miserable food' (v. 5). God was rightly angry, and in judgment

He 'sent venomous snakes among them; they bit the people and many Israelites died' (v. 6).

The narrative avoids graphic details, but it is not hard to imagine the panic that must have spread through the camp. People were dying, and they knew that behind the serpents lay the hand of God. They pleaded with Moses to pray for them. God, in His mercy, responded with some surprising instructions.

> *The LORD said to Moses, 'Make a snake and put it up on a pole; anyone who is bitten can look at it and live.' So Moses made a bronze snake and put it up on a pole. Then when anyone was bitten by a snake and looked at the bronze snake, he lived.*
>
> (Numbers 21:8,9).

Jesus chose this incident to explain the significance of His death. He drew a parallel between the snake that was 'lifted up ... in the desert', and Himself, 'the Son of Man ... lifted up' on a cross (John 3:14). Just as those Israelites who looked at the bronze snake were spared from death, so also 'whoever believes in him shall not perish but have eternal life' (v. 16).

But why this danger of perishing? As Jesus says later on, 'whoever does not believe stands condemned', and 'Whoever believes in the Son has eternal life, but whoever rejects the Son will not see life, for God's wrath remains on him' (vv. 18, 36). By nature, we all stand under God's wrath and condemnation because of our sin, but God has rescued believers through the death of Jesus.

Let us explore some of the implications of penal substitution.

First, it frees us from our guilt in the present. Psychiatrists' waiting-rooms are filled with patients who feel condemned and unlovable, painfully conscious of their failures. The regrets and 'if only's' haunt all of us. But Jesus offers a medicine of which Freud knew nothing. He does not minimize our guilt or pretend it does not exist: He bears it Himself. Jesus' blood has done what no human tears could do. It has washed our consciences clean.

It follows that we shall certainly be pardoned on Judgment Day. Our righteous Judge has punished our sin in Christ, and will not punish the same sins again. As the old hymn asks, 'Will the righteous Judge of men condemn me for that debt of sin which, LORD, was charged on Thee?'[9] Assuredly not.

This biblical teaching offers assurance of a kind not found elsewhere among the world religions. Hinduism's karma, Roman Catholicism's penance, and the prayers of Muslims five times a day all speak of the attempt to amass merit by good deeds. No one can ever be sure they have done enough. Indeed if Allah were truly just, then Paradise should be empty, for Mohammad's teaching offers no explanation of how *sinners* could justly be admitted. But Christians, however conscious they are of evils they have done, can have confidence that they are forgiven and will be welcomed into their Saviour's kingdom. It is by grace we have been saved.

Secondly, penal substitution underscores God's faithfulness and truthfulness. To see how, we need to follow an argument penned by the great fourth-century theologian Athanasius.

Athanasius understood that God cannot simply forgive us for our sin, because He had promised

Adam that sin would bring death: '... you must not eat from the tree of the knowledge of good and evil, for when you eat of it you will surely die' (Genesis 2:17). We are often conscious of the problem of our sin, but consider for a moment what we might call the problem of *forgiving* sin. How can God pardon us without breaking His promise? How can He withhold the death penalty without proving Himself a liar? Indeed, if sin does not bring death, then the serpent becomes the only truth-teller in Eden, for he had asserted, 'You will not surely die' (Genesis 3:4). Athanasius put it this way:

> *It was unthinkable that God, the Father of Truth, should go back upon His word regarding death in order to ensure our continued existence. He could not falsify Himself; what, then, was God to do?*[10]

The answer, of course, is that God upheld His promise to Adam. Sin did bring death, as God had promised – the death of the LORD Jesus in our place.

Let us pause to reflect on what this tells us about God's character. He would rather become incarnate and die than break a single promise. He never speaks and fails to act; He never promises and fails to fulfil.

Consider the difference that this kind of certainty about God's promises might make in our everyday lives. Take, for example, Jesus' instruction that those who give to the needy should do so secretly, so that no one but God will know of their generosity: 'Then your Father, who sees what is done in secret, will reward you' (Matthew 6:4). What a contrast between Jesus' followers and those rich benefactors of our day who insist that a brass plaque should acknowledge their donation! But imagine: you write a cheque to help Christian brothers and sisters in another part of the world. It means denying yourself many luxuries, for it is a large sum of money. And no one knows. You will receive no earthly credit. 'It's worth it,' you think, 'for the one who promised me a heavenly reward is the same LORD who *died* to uphold His promise – I can surely trust Him.'

We might say the same for every one of Jesus' commands, every word that He speaks.

'TO DESTROY THE DEVIL'S WORK'
THE CONQUEST OF EVIL

According to the apostle John, 'The reason the Son of God appeared was to destroy the devil's work' (1 John 3:8). But what is the devil's work, and how does Christ conquer him?

Psalm 2:2 tells us that 'The kings of the earth … gather together against the LORD and against his Anointed One', a hostility seen supremely as the Roman and Jewish authorities conspired to kill Jesus (Acts 4:25–27). Behind these hostile human agencies lie others more sinister, those Paul describes as 'the powers of this dark world' and 'the spiritual forces of evil in the heavenly realms' (Ephesians 6:12).

God is not ultimately threatened, of course, because the devil is a created being and can never rival the power of the Creator. There is no 'god of evil' at war with a 'god of good'.[11] But evil powers are nonetheless real. There is no cosmic dualism, but there is a cosmic mutiny.

This hostility towards God is expressed in hatred of God's people (John 15:18–21): a convert to Christ disowned by her family, a Christian employee marginalized by his colleagues, a Christian student in Africa or Latin America failed in her finals because sexual favours are required for a pass mark. God's people suffer at the hands of the wicked, and their 'enemy the devil prowls around like a roaring lion looking for someone to devour' (1 Peter 5:8).

God's salvation must rescue us not only from the righteous wrath of God (as we discussed in the previous section), but also from these unrighteous evil powers. These two perspectives sit side by side in the Exodus, the defining Old Testament paradigm of deliverance. God's people were spared from His judgment by the sacrifice of a lamb in place of their firstborn sons. They smeared the lamb's blood on the doorposts of their houses, for the LORD had promised, 'when I see the blood, I will pass over you. No destructive plague will touch you' (Exodus 12:13).[12] But the same plague from which God's people were saved fell upon the Egyptians. It was this blow, dealt by God's 'mighty hand', that finally compelled Pharaoh to let the Israelites go (Exodus 6:1; 12:31).

This theme of salvation through conquest appears again and again in the Old Testament. For example:

- At the sound of 300 trumpets, the LORD defeated the Midianite army and saved the Israelites under Gideon (Judges 7).

- Through the slingshot of David, then just a shepherd boy, the LORD defeated the Philistine giant Goliath, and spared His people from slavery (1 Samuel 17).

- By turning the approaching armies of Ammon, Moab and Mount Seir against one another, the LORD delivered Judah under Jehoshaphat (2 Chronicles 20).

Jesus took up the fight against evil throughout His ministry. He cast out evil spirits (e.g. Mark 3:21–28), denounced those whose lives betrayed the devil's family likeness (John 8:44), and spoke of a day when 'the prince of this world [would] be driven out' (John 12:31). That day came with Jesus' crucifixion. There Satan was decisively defeated. There God 'rescued us from the dominion of darkness and brought us into the kingdom of the Son he loves' (Colossians 1:13).

But *how* did Christ accomplish this victory? What did Christ *do* in order to conquer Satan?

Part of the answer lies in his resurrection. Jesus' opponents had conspired to bring about His death (Acts 4:25–27), and behind them lay the hand of Satan, who 'entered Judas' (Luke 22:3). How they must have rejoiced on that first Good Friday, thinking they were rid of Jesus once and for all, only to be confounded three days later. As Jesus ascended to God's right hand, all his enemies were put 'under his feet' (e.g. Ephesians 1:22), fulfilling God's original purposes for humanity (Psalm 8:6). Jesus retraced Adam's steps, resisting temptation where Adam had succumbed (compare Luke 4:1–13 with Genesis 3:1–6), bringing life where Adam had brought death (Romans 5:12–21; 1 Corinthians 15:21–28).

The resurrection cannot be the whole story, however, for the New Testament frequently attributes Jesus' victory directly to the crucifixion: it was 'by his death' (Hebrews 2:14) that Christ destroyed the devil; it was 'by the cross' (Colossians 2:15) that the powers and authorities were disarmed; it was 'by the blood of the Lamb' that Satan was overcome (Revelation 12:11).

Satan's chief weapon is the power to accuse, an insight captured in Zechariah's courtroom vision. God showed him 'Joshua the high priest standing before the angel of the LORD, and Satan standing at his right side to accuse him' (Zechariah 3:1). Satan's case for the prosecution is well-founded, for Joshua stands before God 'dressed in filthy clothes' (Zechariah 3:3), symbolic of the sin that defiles him. As the French theologian Henri Blocher points out, God, 'the righteous Judge of all the earth … cannot refuse to hear the charges the Accuser brings',[13] for they are true. Worse than that, they warrant the death penalty.

This is why Hebrews 2:14 describes the devil as the one 'who holds the power of death'. He has no right or power of his own to punish sinners (and no payment is due to him for their release, a popular but unbiblical idea). It was God who decreed that sinners 'deserve death' (Romans 1:32). Satan takes God's words and wields them as a threat against us. Only by justly removing our penalty could God silence

Satan. Therefore, in biblical thinking, Christ's conquest of Satan depends upon His bearing the punishment we deserve.

There are hints of this already in Zechariah, when Joshua's soiled garments are replaced with clean ones, and he is told that God has 'taken away your sin' (Zechariah 3:4). This is 'symbolic of things to come' when God promises to 'remove the sin of this land in a single day' (vv. 8,9). Thus we need not fear the devil's accusations.

When Satan tempts me to despair
And tells me of the guilt within,
Upward I look, and see him there
Who made an end of all my sin.[14]

The book of Colossians tells a similar story. Here Paul likens the triumph of the cross to a military procession of a kind familiar in the Roman Empire: a victorious soldier would parade the streets, his humiliated captives on display behind him. Similarly, Christ 'made a public spectacle' of the devil and his host, 'triumphing over them by the cross' (Colossians 2:15).

The immediate context in Colossians tells us how the battle was won. Jesus 'cancelled the written code, with its regulations, that was against us and that stood opposed to us; he took it away, nailing it to the cross' (v. 14). The 'written code' refers to the catalogue of charges on which we stand guilty, the very thing Satan had used against us. It was 'cancelled' as Jesus suffered the penalty in our place, and thus the evil 'powers and authorities' were 'disarmed' (v. 15).

'TAKE UP HIS CROSS AND FOLLOW ME' THE CALL TO SERVE AND TO SUFFER

The famous Antarctic explorer, Ernest Shackleton, reportedly placed the following advertisement in a newspaper: 'Men wanted for hazardous journey. Small wages. Bitter cold. Long months of complete darkness. Constant danger. Safe return doubtful. Honour and recognition in case of success.' The stark terms must have dissuaded many from applying, but this was no doubt the intention. Shackleton knew that his own path would be marked by hardship and struggle, and those who followed him must be prepared for the same.

The LORD Jesus was equally clear about the hardships that awaited Him, and no less honest about the likely cost to His followers. Immediately after Peter's confession of Jesus as the Christ, Jesus began to explain that He Himself 'must suffer many things … and that He must be killed' (Mark 8:31), and that anyone wanting to be His disciple 'must deny Himself and take up His cross' (v. 34) and follow Him.

This cross-shaped life of self-denial has two aspects, both revealed in the wider context of this conversation in Mark's Gospel. First, suffering may come our way in the form of persecution, for those opposed to Jesus will be opposed to His followers also. Secondly, we must sometimes choose hardship for the sake of serving our brothers and sisters.

The theme of persecution is introduced by Jesus' teaching about Himself: that He would be 'rejected by the elders, chief priests and teachers of the law', who would in turn 'hand him over to the Gentiles, who will mock him and spit on him, flog him and kill him' (Mark 8:31; 10:33–34). Although Jesus deliberately chose to die (John 10:17,18), fulfilling the purpose of God (Acts 2:23), His death was in another sense brought about by the hostility of those who plotted against Him (e.g. Mark 3:6).

Jesus expected His disciples to face similar opposition: 'You will be handed over to the local councils and flogged in the synagogues' (Mark 13:9). He was right. Only a few weeks later, the apostles were hauled before the council, flogged, and warned never to speak of Jesus again (Acts 5:40). Their response to this is quite amazing: they went away 'rejoicing because they had been counted worthy of suffering disgrace for the Name' (v. 41).

Christians suffer in many parts of the world even today. There were more martyrs in the twentieth century than the previous nineteen centuries combined. Churches are burned to the ground in Indonesia, Sudan, Nigeria; house church leaders are arrested in totalitarian states; Christians are falsely charged and wrongly imprisoned. But their prayers are heard by a LORD who is able to sympathize (Hebrews 4:15), for He himself is 'familiar with suffering' (Isaiah 53:3).

1 Peter is full of instruction for Christians who 'suffer for doing good' and 'are insulted because of the name of Christ' (1 Peter 2:20; 4:14). Peter explains that when Jesus suffered, He was 'leaving you an example, that you should follow in his steps' (1 Peter 2:21). The cross shows us how to suffer in a godly way.

Like Jesus, we must be blameless, for there is nothing commendable about suffering for a crime of which we are guilty (1 Peter 2:20). Like Jesus, we need not fight back, for 'When they hurled their insults at him, he did not retaliate; when he suffered, he made no threats' (1 Peter 2:23). Like Jesus, who 'entrusted himself to him who judges justly' (1 Peter 2:23), we can take comfort in the knowledge that God will finally put things right.

Although we are not to take revenge, the desire for retribution is not wrong in itself. Having taught that Christians must 'not repay anyone evil for evil' (Romans 12:17), the apostle Paul goes on to explain that they need not pursue vengeance because God will do so. 'Do not take revenge, my friends, but leave room for God's wrath, for it is written: "It is mine to avenge; I will repay," says the LORD' (v. 19).[15] Of course, Christians should pray for their enemies (Matthew 5:44), asking that their heavenly Father would forgive them, as Jesus Himself prayed from the cross (Luke 23:34). But even then the penal consequences of sin do not simply disappear; no forgiveness would be possible without Christ's death.

In view of Christ's conquest of evil, it might seem strange that Christians should still suffer at the hands of the ungodly. The reason is that the devil, though defeated, has not yet been destroyed. Historians of World War Two recognize that the fatal blow to Hitler's forces was dealt on D-Day, 6 June 1944, but the Nazis did not finally surrender and lay down their arms until 7 May the following year. In the intervening period, the Nazi forces could still hurt the Allies, but they could not conquer them. Similarly, we can look back and see Satan's defeat, and look forward to the total eradication of evil from God's new creation. In the meantime the devil can still hurt us, but he cannot win.

Christians under persecution should look back and look forward. Back to the cross, where

Christ's death is the pattern for our suffering; forward to 'a living hope ... an inheritance that can never perish, spoil or fade' (1 Peter 1:3,4) secured by His resurrection. Indeed, the 'sufferings of Christ and the glories that would follow' (v. 11) belong together, for even as Jesus went to die He knew He would be raised (e.g. Luke 24:26; Hebrews 12:2).

Like Jesus, Christians can face suffering knowing that their resurrection lies beyond. The apostle Paul had been imprisoned, beaten with rods, stoned, shipwrecked, and had often gone without food and clothing (2 Corinthians 11:23–27). Yet armed with the perspective of Jesus' death and resurrection, he could write that 'our light and momentary troubles are achieving for us an eternal glory that far outweighs them all' (2 Corinthians 4:17), and 'our present sufferings are not worth comparing with the glory that will be revealed in us' (Romans 8:18).

> *Through many dangers, toils, and snares,*
> *I have already come;*
> *'Tis grace has brought me safe thus far,*
> *And grace will lead me home.*[16]

Let us now return to Mark 8, where Jesus invited his would-be disciples to carry their own cross. We have seen that this speaks powerfully to those experiencing persecution. Later in Mark's Gospel, however, when Jesus twice more predicts His passion, He draws out a different implication. 'If anyone wants to be first,' says Jesus, 'he must be the very last, and the servant of all' (Mark 9:35). Again, in response to James and John's request for high positions in the kingdom, Jesus explains that 'whoever wants to become great among you must be your servant, and whoever wants to be first must be slave of all' (Mark 10:43,44). The cross-shaped life is characterized by sacrificial service of others.

Mark Meynell, in his book *Cross-Examined*, points us to a striking illustration of this principle. In the courtyard of Union Seminary in Yeotmal, India, once stood a statue of a tall, dignified figure. At first glance, passers-by would judge him to be someone of importance, for before him knelt a menial slave. But the sculptor has played a trick on us, and the inscription comes as a surprise: 'Jesus washing Peter's feet.'[17]

This act of condescension, described in John 13, points beyond itself to an even greater act of service: Jesus' crucifixion the next morning. John indicates this by sandwiching his description of the foot-washing between two references to Jesus' betrayal (John 13:2, 18–30), and by telling us at the start of the episode that 'the time had come' (v. 1), the long-awaited time of Jesus' death (e.g. John 7:30; 8:20; 12:23,24). Jesus would soon serve His followers in the most costly way possible, giving His life for them.

Jesus goes on to say, 'I have set you an example that you should do as I have done for you' (John 13:15). If our 'LORD and Teacher' (v. 14) humbled Himself to serve others even to the point of death, then we must do the same. Indeed, Jesus assures us, 'Now that you know these things, you will be blessed if you do them' (v. 17).

According to Jesus, such sacrificial service is the essence of love. For just a few verses later he issues His famous command, 'As I have loved you, so you must love one another' (John 13:34). Later that same evening he expands on this: 'Greater love has no-one than this, that he lay down his life for his friends' (John 15:13).

Here is the kind of love by which we will be recognized as disciples of the LORD Jesus. Love for the unlovely; love that crosses boundaries; love that costs us the spare room in our house, the coat off our back, the money in our savings account; perhaps even love that costs our lives. This love is seen nowhere else in the world. Only those who follow Christ crucified can love each other this way.

We find a specific application of this in the Bible's teaching about Christian marriage. Husbands are instructed, 'love your wives, just as Christ loved the church and gave himself up for her' (Ephesians 5:25). A godly husband will not sit back in the armchair while his wife runs around attending to the family's every need; he will take decisions with his wife's interests in mind, rather than just his own; he will take responsibility for the discipline and education of his children. Jesus 'gave himself up' to death for His church, and a godly husband must be prepared to do the same for his wife.

Christ's death provides an example of how to suffer and how to serve. The mistake of the so-called 'moral influence' theory of the atonement, often attributed to the medieval theologians Peter Abelard and Peter Lombard, was to think this a sufficient explanation of the atonement by itself. According to Lombard, 'The death of Christ ... justifies us, inasmuch as through it charity is stirred up in our hearts.'[18] Anselm, a contemporary of Abelard, argued vigorously against this, rightly insisting that Christ's death must provide an objective satisfaction for sin. It is not enough that the cross should merely change *us*, inspiring us to a better life. It must also satisfy the justice and wrath of God.[19]

Accordingly, the New Testament writers seldom mention the exemplary value of Jesus' death in isolation. They always go further. Peter, having laid emphasis on the cross as a pattern for us to follow, goes on to explain that Jesus 'bore our sins' (1 Peter 2:24). This sin-bearing aspect to Jesus' death was 'once for all' (1 Peter 3:18), and is therefore unrepeatable. Again, John reflects on God's gift of his Son, urging His readers that 'since God so loved us, we also ought to love one another' (1 John 4:11). But this follows a statement that Jesus was 'the one who would turn aside [God's] wrath, taking away our sins' (v. 10), something none of us could do.[20]

'CRUCIFIED WITH CHRIST'
OUR PARTICIPATION IN JESUS'
DEATH AND RESURRECTION

Paul says that something incredible took place when the Ephesian Christians believed the gospel, something we may not always think about when describing Christian conversion. They were 'included in Christ' (Ephesians 1:13). The language of being 'in Christ' or 'in him' pervades Paul's letters (e.g. Romans 8:1; 2 Corinthians 5:17; Ephesians 1:3,4,7,11; Philippians 1:1; 3:9), and Christ is also said to be 'in' us by His Spirit (Colossians 1:27). This means that our lives are profoundly connected with the life of Jesus and the events of Calvary. When Christ died, we also died. When He was raised, we were raised. Now He is seated in the heavenly realms, and 'in Christ Jesus' (Ephesians 2:6) we are there too. Theologians describe this as *union with Christ*.

Let us consider the implications of this, beginning with our death in Christ. When Paul writes that he has been 'crucified with Christ' (Galatians 2:20), or that Christians 'have been united with him ... in his death' (Romans 6:5), he speaks of a decisive break with our old lives of sin.

We used to be 'slaves to sin' (Romans 6:6, 17,20). Given the choice between doing the will of God and doing what pleased ourselves, we always opted for what pleased ourselves. We could not do otherwise. But Paul explains that 'anyone who has died has been freed from sin' (v. 7). Now that we have died with Christ, we need 'not let sin reign' (v. 12); its mastery has been broken (v. 14); we 'have been set free from sin and have become slaves to righteousness' (v. 18).

This does not mean Christians live sinless lives – Paul the pastor knows the reality of our ongoing struggles, and he addresses these in Romans 7. But here his focus is on an objective difference that Christ's death has made. Whether we are having a good day or have fallen again into old sinful habits, it remains true that in Christ the power of sin has been broken. The choice to pursue godliness is now open to us. We have real decisions to make:

Do not offer the parts of your body to sin, as instruments of wickedness, but rather offer yourselves to God, as those who have been brought from death to life; and offer the parts of your body to him as instruments of righteousness. (Romans 6:13).

Consider what you have done today with your hands. Perhaps you typed something. Were they words that would honour Christ, or dishonour Him? Perhaps you reached into your pocket for some money. What did you buy? Consider what you have done today with your feet. Where did you walk? Consider what you have done today with your eyes. What did you look at? No doubt we are ashamed of some of our decisions, and for those we are forgiven. But we need not resign ourselves to failure. What will you do with your hands *tomorrow*? Your feet? Your eyes?

Just as you used to offer the parts of your body in slavery to impurity and to ever-increasing wickedness, so now offer them in slavery to righteousness leading to holiness. (Romans 6:19).

Not only have we died, but Paul tells us that we 'have been raised with Christ', and we should set our hearts and minds 'on things above, not on earthly things' (Colossians 3:1,2). At present Christ is hidden from our eyes, and so is the true nature of our life in Him. But both are real, and one day both will be revealed (v. 4).

If you are a believer, then even as you turn the pages of this booklet, you are seated 'in the heavenly realms in Christ Jesus' (Ephesians 2:6). If we could see that we were in God's throne room, we would surely hesitate before slandering a sister in Christ, clicking on a pornographic website, or joining unbelievers in getting drunk at a party. An awareness of our present status in Christ has the power to transform us.

Yet although we have died and been raised with Christ, there remains some unfinished business. God's kingdom has been inaugurated in Christ, and it continues to expand as more and more people 'from every nation, tribe, people and language' (Revelation 7:9) bow the knee to the risen king, but its final consummation must await the Day of Judgment. Christians become a 'new creation' (2 Corinthians 5:17) the moment they believe. But they must still wait for the 'new heaven and a new earth' where God 'will wipe every tear from their eyes' and 'There will be no more death or mourning or crying or pain, for the old order of things has passed away' (Revelation 21:1, 4).

The tension of living as a new person within the 'old order' is felt throughout Romans. We are already 'God's children', and cry out '*Abba*, Father,' yet 'we wait eagerly for our adoption as sons' (Romans 8:15,16,23). We are 'free from the law of sin of death' (v. 2), yet we still sin and we still die! There is a 'now' and a 'not yet' to our Christian experience.

In particular, though we have been raised in the sense described above, we have not yet been raised *bodily*. The body remains in the grip of the sinful nature, 'waging war against the law of my mind' (Romans 7:23). Paul says that the 'body is dead because of sin' (Romans 8:10), and that though we have been crucified already we must continue to 'put to death the misdeeds of the body' (v. 13). The 'redemption of our bodies' (v. 23) still lies in the future.

Nonetheless, our union with Christ in His death guarantees the completion of God's work in us. For 'If we have been united with him like this in his death, we will certainly also be united with him in his resurrection' (Romans 6:5), and 'if the Spirit of him who raised Jesus from the dead is living in you, he who raised Christ from the dead will also give life to your mortal bodies through his Spirit, who lives in you' (Romans 8:11).

The Bible's teaching about union with Christ answers an objection sometimes raised against penal substitution. How could it be right for sinners like us to be counted innocent, while God punished Christ, an innocent third party, instead? Is this not a travesty of justice, of exactly the kind the LORD 'detests' (Proverbs 17:15)? Not at all. Christ is no 'third party', for through our union with Him our sin was counted as His, and his righteousness counted as ours. 'God made him who had no sin to be sin for us, so that in him we might become the righteousness of God' (2 Corinthians 5:21).

Martin Luther perceived a powerful illustration of this in the Bible's teaching that the church is the bride of Christ: 'there is between them a true marriage…it follows that everything they have they hold in common, the good as well as the evil.' If a wealthy businessman were to marry a young girl facing bankruptcy, he would incur her debt, while she would escape destitution. But Luther speaks of a more dramatic contrast: 'Christ is full of grace, life and salvation. The soul is full of sins, death, and damnation. Now let faith come between them and sins, death, and damnation will be Christ's, while grace, life, and salvation will be the soul's.'[21]

WORTHY IS THE LAMB!

Almighty God, we praise You that You so loved the world that You gave Your one and only Son, that whoever believes in Him shall not perish but have eternal life. Thank you that, despite the cost, He willingly drank the cup of Your wrath in our place, and bore our sins in His body on the tree. It is a wonderful blessing to know the forgiveness and free acceptance that comes by His blood.

We praise you that the devil was defeated at Calvary. Please arm us with the shield of faith, that we might extinguish all his flaming arrows.

Help us to silence his accusations, knowing that there is now no condemnation for those who are in Christ Jesus.

We pray for our brothers and sisters around the world who are suffering for their faith. Please strengthen them to follow in the steps of the Lord Jesus and to put their hope in the eternal glory that lies ahead of them.

We pray for ourselves, that we would love one another as the Lord Jesus has loved us. May we be always willing to give whatever we have to serve a brother or sister in need.

Thank you, Father, that You have united us to the Lord Jesus in His death, and that we shall one day be raised bodily with Him. We praise You for liberating us from slavery to sin. Please help us to offer the parts of our body to You as instruments of righteousness.

Together with the thousands of angels who encircle Your throne, we lift our voices and cry: 'Worthy is the Lamb, who was slain, to receive power and wealth and wisdom and strength and honour and glory and praise' (Revelation 5:12).

FURTHER READING

The best place to start is of course the Bible. Why not begin with one of the Gospel accounts of Jesus' death and resurrection (Matthew 26 – 28; Mark 14 – 16; Luke 22 – 24; John 18 – 20)? How do the eyewitness accounts underline Jesus' innocence at his trial? Why is that important? What hints are there that Jesus is in control of events even as He goes to die? What is the significance of that?

Next, turn to one of the New Testament letters, maybe Romans, Hebrews or 1 Peter. Try to pick out passages that are particularly important for explaining the meaning of Jesus' death. How do they relate to the ideas we have outlined in this booklet? What more could we have said?

Finally, delve into the Old Testament to see how Jesus' death was foreshadowed many years beforehand – for example in Exodus 12, Leviticus 16 and Isaiah 53.

After searching the Scriptures for yourself, we'd recommend one of these three books:

- *Cross-Examined* by Mark Meynell is simply written and a brilliant introduction.

- *The Cross of Christ* by John Stott is a classic but a little more stretching.

- *Pierced for our Transgressions* by Steve Jeffery, Mike Ovey and Andrew Sach was written specifically to explain penal substitution and to defend it against recent attacks and misunderstandings. We hope that it will help you to respond biblically to some of the false ideas that are found in the church today.

ENDNOTES

[1] John R.W. Stott, *The Cross of Christ* (Leicester: IVP, 1986), p. 173. For example, the sin of Sodom and Gomorrah was 'so grievous' (Genesis 18:20) that 'the LORD rained down burning sulphur' and 'overthrew those cities and the entire plain, including all those living in the cities' (Genesis 19:24,25). When the Israelites were led into idolatry and sexual immorality by the Moabites, 'the LORD's anger burned against them' and he told Moses to 'Take all the leaders of this people, kill them and expose them in broad daylight before the LORD' (Numbers 25:3,4).

[2] Although Nahum describes God as 'slow to anger' (Nahum 1:3, see also e.g. Exodus 34:6), that only makes His wrath more terrible when it finally appears: 'Who can withstand his indignation? Who can endure his fierce anger? His wrath is poured out like fire; the rocks are shattered before him' (Nahum 1:6). The Bible warns of a future judgment, and those who presume on God's patience are 'storing up wrath' (Romans 2:5) for themselves on that day.

[3] Leviticus 26:33; Deuteronomy 28:15–68; Joshua 23:16; Daniel 9:11–13.

[4] See further Steve Jeffery, Mike Ovey and Andrew Sach, *Pierced for Our Transgressions: Rediscovering the Glory of Penal Substitution* (Nottingham: IVP / Illinois: Crossway, 2007), pp. 50,60.

[5] See for example Matthew 8:16,17; Luke 22:37; John 12:38; Acts 8:32,33; Romans 15:20,21.

[6] The idea that Jesus was 'cursed' for us, found also in Galatians 3:13, was important to several early Christian writers. For example, the second century theologian Justin Martyr wrote that 'the Father of all wished His Christ for the whole human family to take upon Him the curses of all' *(Dialogue with Trypho, xcv)*. Similar statements are found in Eusebius of Caesarea, *Proof of the Gospel*, 10.1 and Hilary of Poitiers, *Homily on Psalm 53 (54)*, 13.

[7] See also Joel 2:31; Amos 5:18,20; Zephaniah 1:14,15.

[8] Keith Getty / Stuart Townend, 'In Christ Alone'. Copyright © 2001 Thankyou Music. Adm. by worshiptogether.com songs excl. UK & Europe, adm. by kingswaysongs.com tym@kingsway.co.uk

[9] Augustus M. Toplady 1740-78, 'From whence this fear and unbelief?' Taken from *Christian Hymns* (Bryntirion, Bridgend: Evangelical Movement of Wales, 1977).

[10] Athanasius, *On the Incarnation*, VI.

[11] Paul's descriptions of the devil as 'The god of this age' (2 Corinthians 4:4) and 'the ruler of the kingdom of the air' (Ephesians 2:2) are sarcastic titles, and certainly not intended to dignify him with deity. He is a creature (Genesis 3:1), not the Creator, and his sphere of authority is subordinate to God's (Job 1).

[12] This deliverance from God's judgment through the blood of a lamb was celebrated throughout Israel's history in an annual Passover meal. Jesus himself ate the Passover with His disciples on the eve of His death, but interpreted it in a shocking new way: '...this is my body ... This is my blood' (Mark 14:22,24). Jesus understood his crucifixion as the fulfilment of Israel's deliverance from Egypt. As Paul later commented, 'Christ, our Passover lamb, has been sacrificed' (1 Corinthians 5:7).

[13] Henri A.G. Blocher, 'Agnus Victor: The Atonement as Victory and Vicarious Punishment', in John G. Stackhouse (ed.), *What does it Mean to be Saved?* (Grand Rapids: Baker, 2002), p. 83.

[14] Charitie L. Bancroft 1841-1923, 'Before the Throne of God Above'. Taken from *Christian Hymns*.

[15] This does not mean that it is wrong for an employer to sack a dishonest employee or a court to sentence a murderer, for Paul envisages that God may use human 'governing authorities' (Romans 13:1) as instruments of his wrath in advance of the final Judgment Day.

[16] John Newton 1822-1895, 'Amazing Grace'. Taken from *Christian Hymns*.

[17] Mark Meynell, *Cross-Examined: The Life-Changing Power of the Death of Jesus* (Leicester: IVP, 2005), p. 164.

[18] Peter Lombard, *Book of Sentences*, iii, Dist. xix.1, quoted in Stott, *Cross of Christ*, p. 218.

[19] Anselm did not quite put it this way. Within his feudal thought-world, it was God's honour that needed to be satisfied by substitutionary obedience, not his justice by substitutionary penalty. Thus he departed subtly from the biblical doctrine of penal substitution.

[20] Our quotation is from the NIV footnote, which reflects a more accurate translation of the Greek word *hilasterion*. See further Jeffery, Ovey and Sach, *Pierced for Our Transgressions*, pp. 82–85.

[21] Martin Luther, *The Freedom of a Christian*, in *Three Treatises*, trans. W.A. Lambert, Rev. H.J. Grimm (Philadelphia: Fortress, 1970), p. 286. The analogy between marriage and union with Christ is not perfect, for Christ does not merely share our debt, offering to pay it with us. Rather, He pays it for us.